Making a Difference

RECYCLING

Materials

Sue Barraclough

SEA-TO-SEA

Mankato Collingwood London

This edition first published in 2008 by
Sea-to-Sea Publications
1980 Lookout Drive
North Mankato
Minnesota 56003

Copyright © Sea-to-Sea Publications 2008

Printed in the United States of America

Library of Congress
Cataloging in Publication Data

Barraclough, Sue.
   Recycling materials / by Sue Barraclough.
      p.cm.
   Includes index.
   ISBN 978-1-59771-108-1
   1. Refuse and refuse disposal--Juvenile literature. 2. Recycling (Waste, etc.)--Juvenile
literature. I. Title.

TD792.B37 2007
363.72'82--dc22

                                                    2006053197

9 8 7 6 5 4

Published by arrangement with the Watts Publishing Group Ltd, London.

Original concept devised by Sue Barraclough and Jemima Lumley.

Editor: Adrian Cole
Designer: Jemima Lumley
Art director: Jonathan Hair
Special photography: Mark Simmons (except where listed below)
Consultant: Helen Peake, Education Officer at
   The Recycling Consortium, Bristol

Acknowledgments:
The author and publisher wish to thank Helen Peake and the staff at
The Recycling Consortium. Crystal Paving: 13br, 26br. Green Glass
(www.greenglass.co.uk): 13cl and bl. Paperpod (www.paperpod.co.uk): 27b.
Patagonia (www.patagonia.com): 17br, 26tr. Remarkable Pencils Ltd
(www.remarkable.co.uk): 22 and 26cl. Images on 7c, 7bl, 7br, 9t, 12b, 19b,
25t supplied by the national Recycle Now campaign (for more information
on recycling visit www.recyclenow.com). Chris Fairclough: 15t, 25b.
© Digital Vision: 24. Neil Thomson: 13tl. Bob Daemmrich/Image
Works/Topfoto: 14b. Eastcott-Momatiuk/Topfoto: 19t. David R. Frazier/Image
Works/Topfoto: 11c, 11b. Photri/Topfoto: 16b. Novelis: 15c, 15b. Revolve
(www.revolve-uk.com): 27tl.

Special thanks to Connie, James, Romi, Ruby, and Vincent for taking part.

Contents

Is it garbage?

All of these things can be recycled. The materials they are made from can be used again. Recycling helps save energy and reduce garbage.

Some materials are used to make the same thing. Other materials are used to make a different object.

Plastic

Paper

None of these things should go into a trash can. They should be recycled.

Glass

Metal

Fruit and vegetable waste

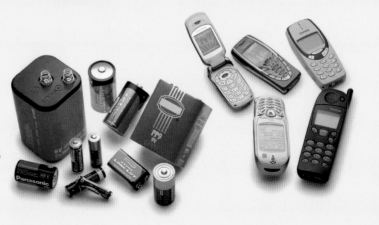

⚠️ **Dangerous waste**

Batteries and cellphones contain dangerous chemicals that need to be specially recycled.

Making compost

Fruit and vegetable waste can be recycled in a compost bin or a wormery. The waste changes into compost that can be used to grow more fruit and vegetables.

Plant materials break down naturally. Heat and creatures, such as worms, are part of the process.

Waste in a compost bin becomes moldy and smelly. The smell means the waste is breaking down. It is changing into something useful.

The plant materials change into compost. It is full of goodness that plants need to grow. People use compost to grow seeds.

Recycling paper

All of these things are made of paper. They can all be recycled.

Printer paper

Magazines

Newspapers

Junk mail

Craft paper

Greetings cards

Wrapping paper

Shredded paper

Paper bags

Waste paper is sorted
and chopped up.
Then it is cleaned
with hot water and
mashed up. This
changes it into a paper
porridge called pulp.

Then the pulp is
squeezed and squashed
together. It is dried and
pressed flat and smooth.

The recycled paper
is rolled up and then
used to make more
paper things.

Recycling glass

These glass bottles and jars can be recycled. Some recycling schemes collect glass from homes. Some people put glass into bottle banks.

All of the glass is taken to a recycling center where they collect lots of materials. The glass is sorted out into different colors.

Then the glass is crushed, melted, and shaped to make new glass bottles and jars.

Different uses for recycled glass

Sometimes the glass is made into other things.

Glass paving

Glass jewelry

Recycling metal

Aluminum and steel are metals used to make soda cans. Steel is also used to make food cans.

GLASS

ALUMINUM CANS

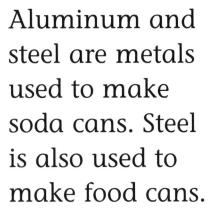

What you can do

Find out if your school has a recycling scheme. You may be able to help sort out the recycling.

Recycled metal is sorted out, crushed, and melted down. The metal can be shaped in lots of ways.

The metal may be used to make more cans. Sometimes it is used to make parts for cars, machines, and airplanes.

Recycling plastic

There are lots of different kinds of plastic. Most of them are made from oil. Plastic can be thin and flexible, hard and strong, or soft and squashy.

Be a plastic spotter!

Look at the number symbols in the triangles. Each one shows what type of plastic the object is made from. There are seven different symbols to look for.

Plastics with the numbers 1 and 2 are most likely to be recycled.

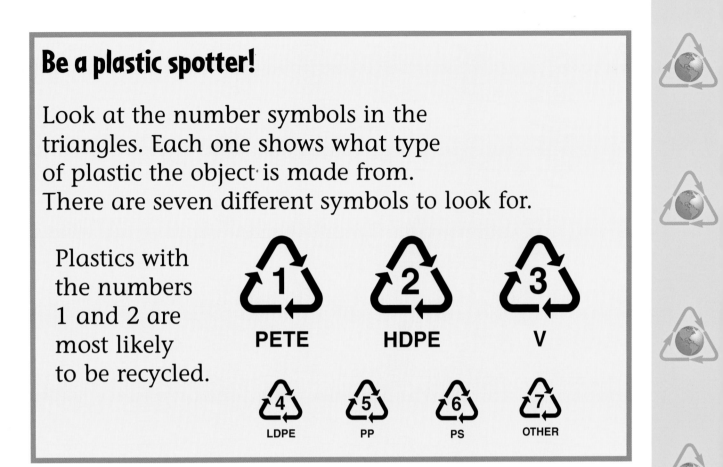

1 PETE
2 HDPE
3 V
4 LDPE
5 PP
6 PS
7 OTHER

Number 1 (PETE or PET) plastic bottles can be recycled to make lots of things. Some are recycled to make fluffy fleeces.

Fifteen bottles will make one fleece.

Ways to recycle

Recycling is simple. Many places have a collection scheme. You leave your materials outside your home in a box. The recyclers come and take them away.

People also take their materials to a
special recycling center. They put
each item into a different container.

Sorting out recycling

If you know where each material goes, you can sort them out easily. Even the youngest members of your family will put things in the right place!

Choose a container to keep your recycling in. You could use boxes like the ones below, or a bag.

Paper

Metal

Glass

Write labels or draw pictures to show everyone what to put in there.

Buy recycled

Buying things that are made from recycled materials is very important too.

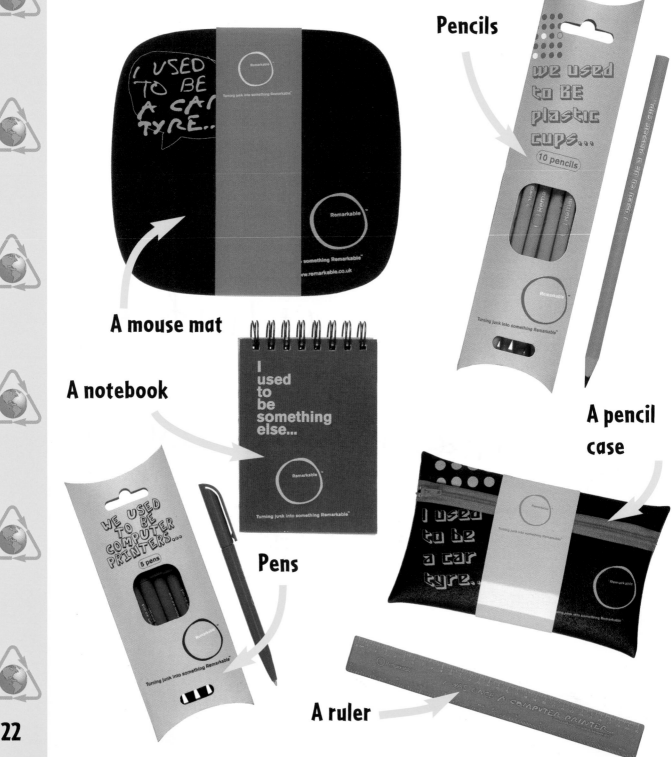

Pencils

We used to be plastic cups...
10 pencils

A mouse mat

I USED TO BE A CAR TYRE...

A notebook

I used to be something else...
Turning junk into something Remarkable

A pencil case

I used to be a car tyre...

Pens

WE USED TO BE COMPUTER PRINTERS...
5 pens

A ruler

WAS ONCE A COMPUTER PRINTER

Recycled paper

Did you know?

You can buy toilet paper made from recycled paper. Some playground equipment is made from recycled plastic.

Recycled plastic

Recycle it safely

There are some materials that must be recycled very carefully. Batteries, computers, and cellphones have parts that can be used again.

Dangerous materials are collected and sorted out separately. They are taken to special recycling centers.

Old cellphones and computers have their parts recycled. Some can be repaired and reused.

What you can do

Try not to use normal batteries. Use rechargeable batteries instead.

Batteries contain dangerous chemicals so they need to be specially recycled.

Recycled material?

Can you guess what material has been recycled to make each thing?

1

2

I USED TO BE A PLASTIC CUP.

10 pencils

3

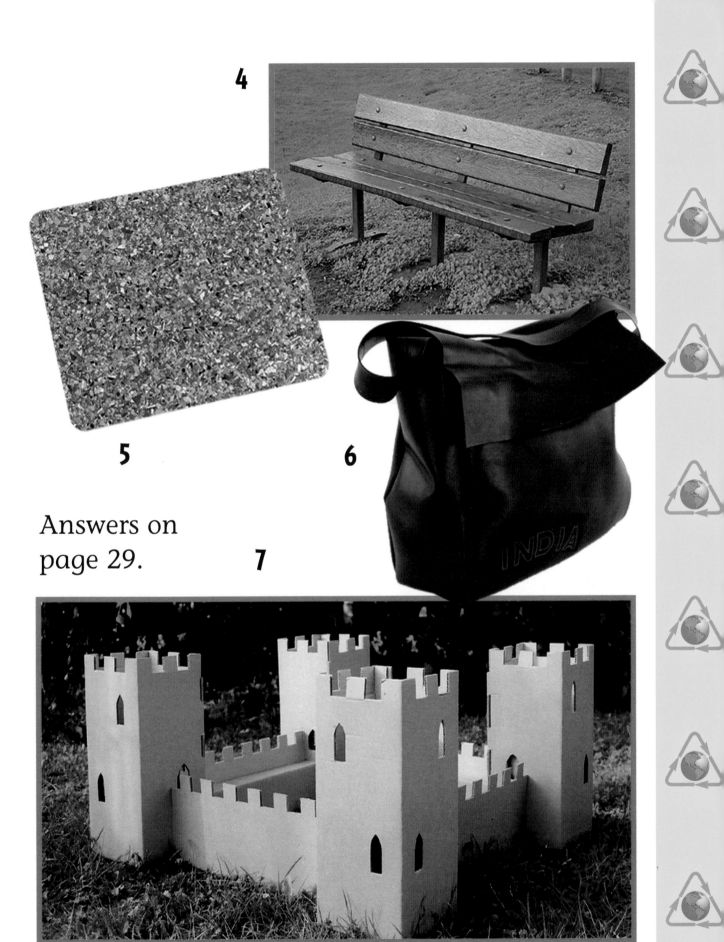

4

5

6

Answers on
page 29.

7

Find out more

Ask an adult to call your city hall to find out about the services they provide for recycling, or visit their website. They should be able to give you details of their box collection scheme, if they have one, and how to find recycling centers. Try to recycle fewer things by reducing rubbish and reusing things.

www.eia.doe.gov/kids/ energyfacts/saving/recycling
The U.S. Government Energy Information Administration's site for children has comprehensive information about all aspects of recycling paper and glass.

www.kid-at-art.com
All about creative ways to recycle by making art.

www.earth911.org/ master.asp
Click on the "Kids" link for educational children's activities and information on every aspect of recycling.

www.thinkcans.com
A website on recycling aluminum cans.

www.glassforever.co.uk
A user-friendly website packed with facts and information about glass packaging and recycling glass processes.

www.recyclezone.org.uk
Waste Watch website with games, information and activities on recycling, and the 3Rs (Reducing, Reusing and Recycling).

Glossary

Bottle bank—a container for storing glass to be recycled.

Compost—plant materials that have broken down. People use compost to help plants grow.

Compost bin—a container used to store kitchen and garden waste where it breaks down to make compost.

Material—the substance something is made from. For example, paper is made from a material called wood.

Recycle—when you use something again or make it into something new.

Recycling collection scheme—a system where materials to be recycled are collected from outside homes.

Wormery—a special container to hold worms and waste. Most kitchen and garden waste, and torn paper and cardboard can be added. It is broken down by the worms.

Answers to the quiz on pages 26–27: 1—the fleece is made from PET (number 1) plastic bottles; 2—the outside of the pencils is made from plastic cups; 3—the paving is made from recycled glass; 4—the bench is made from recycled plastic; 5—the mouse mat is made from recycled drinks cartons; 6—the bag is made from rubber from tire inner tubes; 7—the toy castle is made from recycled paper.

Index

About this book

Making a Difference: Recycling Materials encourages children to help recycle, and think carefully about the value of materials and how they can be used again. Discuss with children the idea that the world has limited resources, and that if we waste them, they cannot be replaced and may eventually run out.

Explore the idea that it is easy to throw something into a trash can and send it off to a landfill site, but that it is important for us all to realize that if we carry on this way we will run out of space to bury it all.

Page 8 encourages children to see that the rotting process is a natural way to recycle some materials.
Pages 10–17 encourage children to look carefully at materials and to notice similarities and differences. It also helps them understand the process of recycling.
Page 18 looks at the idea of sorting and storing materials for recycling. Children can play an active part in the process.
Page 22 encourages children to spot recycling symbols in shops.
Pages 24–25 can be used to explore the idea that certain things contain dangerous materials, so they need to be recycled responsibly.
Use **pages 26–27** to promote the idea that we can buy goods made of different recycled materials.